crafting *with*
handmade paper

PAPER

My, what a simple thing you are
so useful
you and your wonderful whiteish color.
Paper, I really use you.

Will Hercher, age 11.
1996

GLOUCESTER MASSACHUSETTS

QUARRY
BOOKS

crafting *with*
handmade
paper

GREAT PROJECTS TO MAKE *with* **BEAUTIFUL PAPERS**

Gail Hercher

Rockport Publishers would like to thank the following people for their contributions to *Crafting with Handmade Paper.*

Kindra Clineff, pg. 50

Martha Everson, pgs. 74, 108

JG&R Associates, pg. 67

Elaine Koretsky, pgs. 33, 37, 41, 45, 49, 57, 61, 73, 83, 89, 95

Michael Lafferty, pg. 96

Mary McCarthy

Brian Thomas

Robert C. Williams American Museum of Papermaking, pg. 77

Jessica Wrobel, pg. 96

First published in the United States of America by
Rockport Publishers, Inc.
33 Commercial Street
Gloucester, Massachusetts 01930-5089
Telephone: (978) 282-9590
Facsimile: (978) 283-2742
www.rockpub.com

ISBN 1-56496-710-7

10 9 8 7 6 5 4 3 2 1

Design: Leeann Leftwich
Art Direction and Photostyling: Cathy Kelley
Cover Image: Kevin Thomas

Printed in China.

contents

introduction

Beautiful handmade papers from around the world are available from paper stores and art supply stores and catalogs. Delicate Japanese mulberry papers, sturdy Nepalese daphne papers, Egyptian papyrus, Mexican bark paper, Italian and French rag papers, Indian floral papers, and many others offer surfaces that are colorful, highly textured, and much more interesting than ordinary machine-made sheets.

Artists, graphic designers, photographers, craftspeople, architects, bookbinders, interior designers, and desktop publishers are incorporating handmade paper in their work as the global economy enables the international importation of papers. With a phone call to a catalog, an interior designer can order handmade bamboo wallpaper from the Philippines!

Some people advance their interest in handmade papers by learning to make their own. They take workshops, read books, or study at one of the many art schools and universities that offer degrees in papermaking and the book arts. Why is this happening in the computer age, when futurists are predicting that books and paper will disappear? I believe it's because handmade objects affirm the importance of the individual and reveal a collective yearning for past values such as patience, quality, craftsmanship, solitude, and quiet. The deckled edge, rose petals, and burnished or wrinkled surfaces of handmade papers reflect these values and show the hand of the individual.

I was drawn to hand papermaking after an illness associated with printmaking chemicals. I wanted to use a clean medium that did not pollute the environment or my health. (I also abandoned oil-based inks and solvents.) I have explored many avenues with paper—weaving, bookbinding, making clothes and hats, origami, basketry, printmaking—and have even sold designs to a commercial wallpaper manufacturer. Today, I am particularly interested in using recycled materials to make paper, which I use in baskets, books, and collages.

As this book illustrates, every culture has developed its own way of using handmade paper—layered and sewn as cloth, glued for transparent effects, laminated for strength. Each chapter focuses on a paper from a particular country and explains its use and history.

Of ecological interest are the papers from developing countries that are practicing sustainable living practices and experimenting with farm waste products in papermaking. Costa Rica, the Ukraine, Israel, and the Philippines are making great strides in this direction. Unfortunately, in the United States—the biggest maker, user, and waster of paper—commercial paper mills are making slow progress toward bringing recycled paper to market at a competitive price. The Green Field Paper Company, a small mill in San Diego, however, makes beautiful handmade sheets from junk mail on a commercial basis. As increased emphasis is placed on resource recovery, many more recycled papers will be seen.

I hope you enjoy making these crafts and learning about hand-made papers from around the world.

Gail Hercher

MATERIALS & *supplies*

by Mary McCarthy

In addition to various kinds of paper, you will need a few other materials and supplies to complete the projects in this book.

Adhesives

Paper is adhered to a mat using glue or paste. For the projects described in this book, polyvinyl acetate (PVA) is recommended. It is white, dries clear, and can be thinned with water. You can substitute PVA with other white paper glues. You can also use wheat paste, rice paste, YES paste, or paste made from cornstarch. If you want to mix your own paste, you can find recipe books that show you how.

Thread

You will need to sew a binding on some of the projects in this book. Professional binders use linen thread, which is strong but rather expensive. As a substitute, you can use thick cotton thread, embroidery silk, or even dental floss if the project is small. A variety of ribbons, cords, or twine can add color to your spine. Avoid using sewing thread, which breaks easily.

Tools

This list includes all the tools you could possibly need to complete every project in this book. Not every tool is required for each project; some call for just a pair of scissors and a bone folder. For other more complicated, projects you will need an awl, sewing needle, and strong thread.

1. Hand drill with various bits or an electric drill
2. Bone folder
3. Clamps or metal art clips
4. Assorted craft needles
5. Pencil
6. Hole punch
7. Awl
8. Glue brush
9. Scissors
10. Utility knife or mat knife
11. Paintbrushes

HOW TO MAKE *corners*

by Mary McCarthy *Making Books by Hand*

For several of the projects in this book, cover boards or matboards are wrapped with either cloth or paper. The type of material you use, whether it is thin paper or cloth, thick or brittle paper, or standard cloth or paper, will determine how you wrap the corners of the boards. It requires practice to make neat corners. Take time to study the three methods of wrapping corners described on the pages that follow. For each method, make sure you cut the material no closer than ¼" (.5 cm) to the corners of the board.

METHOD *one*

For Thin Paper or Cloth

Cut off the corners of your material at a diagonal fold, and glue one side of the material down on the board.

Use a bone folder to press the paper down at a slight angle over the corner.

Glue and fold the paper on the adjacent side in the same way.

METHOD *two*

For Thick or Brittle Paper

Cut off the corners of your paper at a diagonal fold, and glue one side down on the board. Then, with scissors, cut a straight line from the fold of the paper that extends to the corner of the board.

With a bone folder or a finger, tuck the small triangular piece you have just created around the corner onto the lip of the adjacent side. Snip off the peak that has formed with scissors as shown.

Glue and fold the adjacent side down on the board.

METHOD *three*

For Cloth or Paper

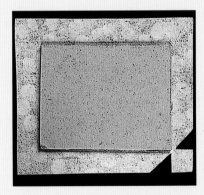

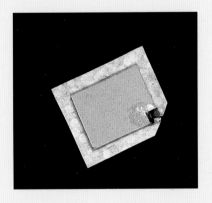

Cut a square into the cloth or paper as shown. Cut carefully so that one corner of the square remains attached to the material.

Glue and fold the square over the inside of the board.

Glue and fold the adjacent sides of the material down on the inside of the board.

PAPERS from all over the world can be artfully combined to make unusual invitations that intrigue prospective guests. Earth-tone papers for a rehearsal dinner in New Mexico, lavender floral papers for a spring shower, white sheer unryu paper with gold and silver flecks for a wedding—each communicates the mood of a special occasion. In these projects, text is printed on a computer or by a professional printer, then combined with handmade papers. After deciding on the envelope size, experiment with sample invitations. Have fun, but keep the design relatively simple—making one invitation may not take long, but making 100 will.

When the design is complete, carefully calculate how much paper is needed for the total project or sketch how many pieces can be cut per sheet. Staff at paper stores are usually helpful in making this calculation; they may also give a discount for quantity orders.

Ideas for three styles of invitations are given—but feel free to alter or combine them to suit your own vision.

SPECIAL OCCASION *invitations*

TIPS

Many thin, smooth handmade papers can be used in a computer printer—just make sure the ink doesn't rub off. Professional printers will sometimes agree to print on handmade paper. In either case, test first.

Invite a friend over for wine and make the invitations together.

The key to a successful invitation is starting with the envelope and working backward, making sure that all the pieces—invitation, response card, map, etc.—fit inside. Always buy or make the envelope first. Templates for three envelope sizes are included at the back of this book (see pg. 100).

Choosing the Paper

This simple style can be very elegant. Choose a good-quality stock for the inside sheet, a handmade cover sheet, and a thin tissue for the inside. Use computer graphics to add images. Make the envelope first, using the same paper as either the inside sheet or the cover sheet. Make the invitation to fit the envelope.

the PAMPHLET-STYLE *invitation*

1

2

Materials · *makes two invitations and two envelopes* · 1 sheet 8 ½" x 11" (22 cm x 28 cm) good-quality computer printer paper or a smooth, thin handmade paper (for invitation) · 2 sheets 8 ½" x 11" (22 cm x 28 cm) thick tan Bhutanese paper (for cover of invitation and envelope) · 1 sheet 8 ½" x 11" (22 cm x 28 cm) thin pink Bhutanese paper (for invitation and envelope liner) · glue stick · 2 feet waxed linen thread, embroidery thread, or narrow ribbon · metal ruler for measuring and tearing · scissors · pencil · sewing needle · computer printer (or your own handwriting)

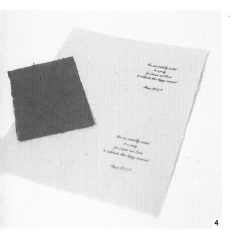

4

STEP 1 Using the template from the back of this book (see Template section, pg. 100), trace an A2 envelope shape onto envelope paper and cut out. Trace this pattern again onto contrasting paper to make the envelope liner. Remove side flaps from pink liner paper. **STEP 2** Glue liner onto envelope with glue stick (not wet glue, as paper will wrinkle). Fold in flaps; glue envelope into shape with glue stick. **STEP 3** Cut one sheet of cover paper in half. Take one half sheet, 5 ½" x 8 ½" (14 cm x 22 cm), and fold in half to make the invitation cover. **STEP 4** Print text by running invitation paper through computer. Two invitations will fit on one sheet. Cut in half. Fold so that text is on the inside. **STEP 5** Cut a piece of envelope liner paper to the same size as the invitation, 4 ¼" x 5 ½" (11 cm x 14 cm).

TIP
One quarter of an 8 ½" x 11" (22 cm x 28 cm) sheet fits into an A2 envelope.

Pamphlet Stitch

 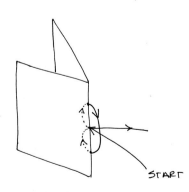

START

STEP 6 Assemble in the following order from inside to outside: invitation, thin paper, thick cover paper. Sew together with pamphlet stitch according to diagram.

STEP 7 Tear two rectangular shapes of tan and pink. Glue onto cover with glue stick.

TIP

Use a hand-carved eraser stamp or commercial rubber stamp to create an embossed design on the front of the invitation. Using Color Box Ink, stamp image onto cover. Sprinkle with embossing powder. Melt with heat gun.

the LAYERED invitation

Materials · makes three invitations and three envelopes · 1 sheet Indian floral paper, 22" x 30" (56 cm x 76 cm) · 1 sheet Japanese unryu paper, 22" x 30" (56 cm x 76 cm) · 1 sheet card stock, 8 ½" x 11" (22 cm x 28 cm) · raffia · pencil · scissors · glue stick · needle · bone folder

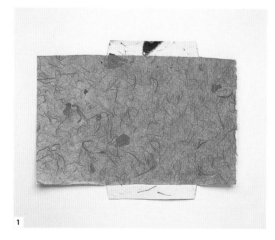

1

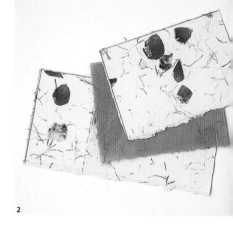

2

3

4

STEP 1 Trace A6 envelope pattern (see Template section, pg. 100) onto Indian floral paper and Japanese unryu paper (for liner). Cut out; remove side flaps from unryu liner. Crease with bone folder and glue together into envelope shape. **STEP 2** Cut out two pieces of Indian floral paper, one the size of the envelope and the other about 3" (8 cm) longer. Cut Japanese unryu paper the size of the envelope. **STEP 3** Print text on card stock or paper the size of the envelope. **STEP 4** Stack in the following order, top to bottom: smaller floral paper, unryu, text paper, longer piece of floral paper. Wrap extra length around to front. Sew pamphlet stitch (see page 22).

Choosing the Paper

This style of invitation uses the pamphlet stitch on the top surface of the invitation instead of the spine. It offers many opportunities to go wild with sheer and opaque papers, ribbons, raffia, and cutout designs. The key is an imaginative choice of papers and a sensitivity to the juxtaposition of ragged and straight edges.

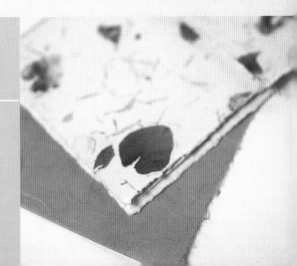

the WRAPPED *invitation*

Materials · *makes four invitations and four envelopes* · 1 sheet Thai floral paper for outside wrapping, 22" x 30" (56 cm x 76 cm) · 1 sheet Japanese coordinating lightweight paper for liner and envelope, 22" x 30" (56 cm x 76 cm) · 1 sheet card stock for invitation printing, 8 1/2" x 11" (22 cm x 28 cm) · raffia · pencil · scissors · glue stick · bone folder

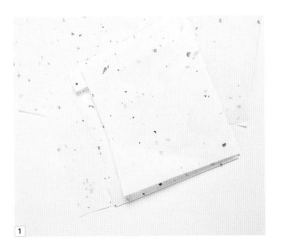

1

STEP 1 Cut out square envelope template (see Template section, pg. 100) and trace onto lightweight paper. Cut out envelope and glue into shape with glue stick. **STEP 2** Print invitation text on card stock the same size as envelope.

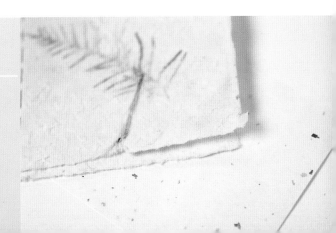

Choosing the Paper

This invitation uses the simplest technique-wrapping-no sewing or gluing necessary. The text is surrounded by beautiful handmade paper, tied with raffia, and placed inside an exquisite envelope made of lightweight bark paper. Another piece of bark paper veils the invitation inside. This technique can be utilized on any scale.

4

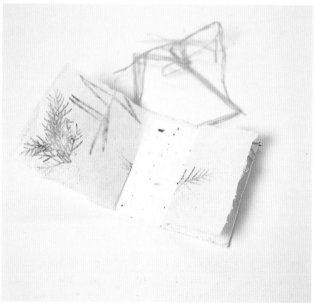

STEP 3 Cut invitation veil (liner) out of the same paper as the envelope. The liner should be the same size as envelope. **STEP 4** Cut a piece of Thai floral paper three times as long as the invitation. Fold into thirds. Fold the first third in half as shown on dotted line. This designates the front of the invitation. Place veil on top of invitation, wrap floral paper around the text with the veil, and tie with raffia.

TIP
Square envelopes require extra postage. Check with the post office for correct amount to avoid having your lovely invitations returned.

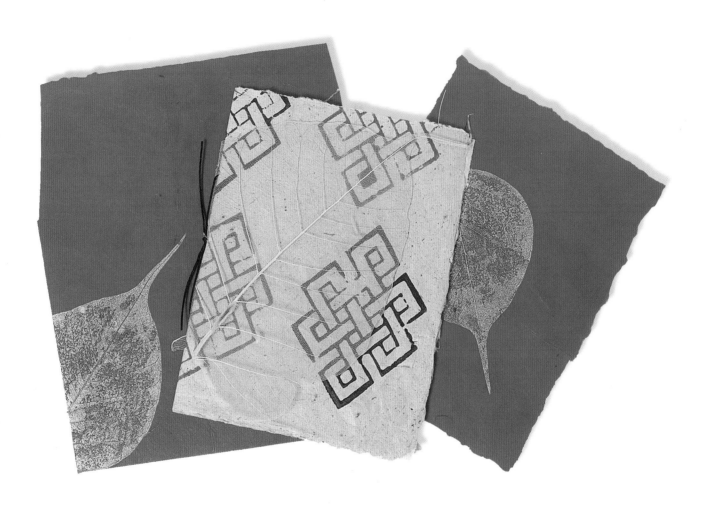

An Invitation for Any Occasion

Create unique invitations to coordinate with a theme, be it an Asian dinner party, a black-tie affair, or a simple get-together. Experiment with different textures of paper, ribbons, and cords.

HANDMADE Indian papers, with their botanical inclusions and long history, are ideal for window treatments. Sandwich a floral paper between two picture frames and hang it in a window to both grace and preserve your privacy. Alternatively, hang a pleated botanical paper from clips on a tension curtain rod. Because Indian papers are so inexpensive, you can change "curtains" frequently—to create a mood, to refresh your spirits, to alter the room's decor. The variety of papers available makes for a multitude of possibilities.

INDIA

FRAMED WINDOW *hanging*

Materials · 2 identical picture frames, with glass · 1 sheet Indian floral paper, 22" x 30" (56 cm x 76 cm) · 1 sheet acetate, 18" x 24" (46 cm x 61 cm) · acrylic paint for coloring frames · paintbrush · glue stick · Velcro tape · Four ¹¹/₁₆" (16.5 mm) screw eyes · wire or cord for hanging · screwdrivers · ruler · pencil · scissors · utility knife · glue brush · soft, clean rag · electric drill

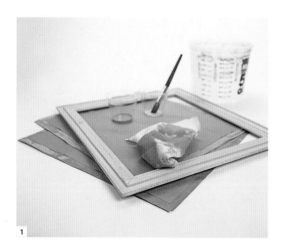

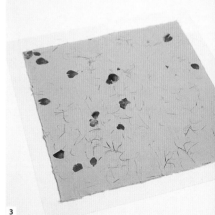

GETTING STARTED Remove all hardware and glass from the picture frames. Clean all parts thoroughly. Mix paint colors to coordinate with the floral paper to be used.

STEP 1 Thin the coordinating paint a little with water, paint onto frames (front and back) with a brush, and rub with a rag to create a distressed look. **STEP 2** Using the glass as a pattern, cut a piece of acetate the same size. **STEP 3** Tear the Indian paper about 1" (3 cm) smaller than the acetate on all sides. Attach to acetate using a glue stick at the top. Set the acetate/paper in the frame and anchor in place.

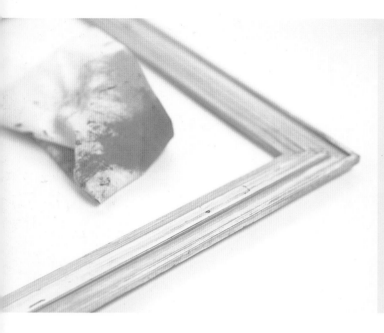

TIP
The distressed look is achieved by painting on several layers of color and rubbing in between each with the rag. This gives the frame an aged appearance that complements paper from an ancient traditional culture.

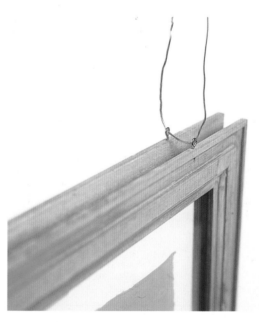

4

STEP 4 Attach the frames to each other with Velcro tape. Predrill the screw eye holes with an electric drill. Attach screw eyes to the top of both frames. Run a wire or cord through. Hang framed paper from top of window frame.

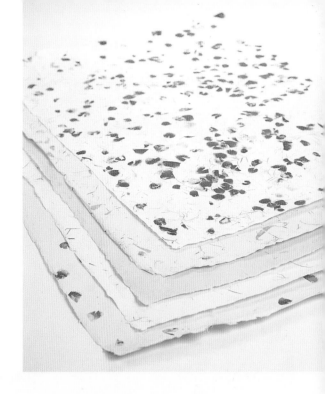

About the Paper

India's handmade paper industry almost disappeared when the British introduced machine-made paper. Fortunately, Mahatma Gandhi and governmental agencies revived this craft, and today villagers make many kinds of paper. Some use recycled cotton fiber and indigenous plants, but the most popular sheets feature botanical inclusions such as marigolds, roses, and grass (see illustration). These papers are widely available through art supply catalogs and at paper stores.

Interior of a hand paper mill in Pondicherry, India.

Pleated Curtain

Fold (pleat) the piece of Indian floral paper in eighths. Slide curtain clips onto a tension cafe curtain rod and attach them to the paper. Voilà! Instant curtains.

CHANGE the appearance of any room quickly, inexpensively, and beautifully! Or redo a room with botanical paper for a special event—perhaps roses for Valentine's Day or pine sprigs for Christmas. Thai artisans produce a wide range of papers with embedded plant materials (flowers, ferns, leaves, grasses, etc.) that make striking tiles. These are so easy to make that you can decide in the morning to create a new interior by evening. The secret is the Velcro dots—they don't leave marks and will hold the tiles in place until the next time you want a change.

THAILAND

BOTANICAL WALL *tiles*

Materials · glue · botanical paper, 22" x 30" (56 cm x 76 cm) · mat board · Velcro dots · matte gel medium · ruler · pencil · utility knife · white glue · container · brush · scissors · weights (such as books or bricks)

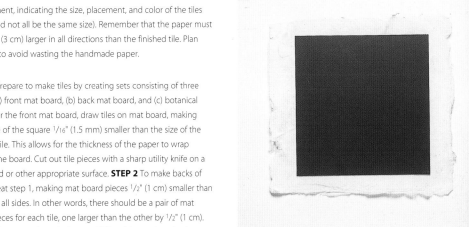

TIP
Get scrap mat board from a local framer. When cutting mat board, use a utility knife and score several times on each line until cut through. Do not attempt to cut through board in one cut.

GETTING STARTED Measure the wall area to be tiled. Sketch the arrangement, indicating the size, placement, and color of the tiles (they need not all be the same size). Remember that the paper must be cut 1" (3 cm) larger in all directions than the finished tile. Plan carefully to avoid wasting the handmade paper.

STEP 1 Prepare to make tiles by creating sets consisting of three pieces: (a) front mat board, (b) back mat board, and (c) botanical paper. For the front mat board, draw tiles on mat board, making each side of the square 1/16" (1.5 mm) smaller than the size of the finished tile. This allows for the thickness of the paper to wrap around the board. Cut out tile pieces with a sharp utility knife on a cardboard or other appropriate surface. **STEP 2** To make backs of tiles, repeat step 1, making mat board pieces 1/2" (1 cm) smaller than fronts on all sides. In other words, there should be a pair of mat board pieces for each tile, one larger than the other by 1/2" (1 cm). **STEP 3** Cut or tear botanical paper 1" (3 cm) larger than the front tile piece on all sides.

4

5

STEP 4 Spread glue on the botanical paper. Press front mat board piece onto paper. Trim corners of paper. Turn in four sides, making neat corners (see How to Make Corners, pg.14). Spread glue on back mat board piece. Press down onto back surface of tile front. Let dry under weights. Complete all tiles for wall. Keep under weights.

STEP 5 Put a Velcro dot on each corner of tile back. Peel paper off dots and attach to wall. Draw light pencil lines with level on wall, if necessary, to keep tiles straight and plumb.

TIP
Wall Tiles can be brushed to remove dust. For further protection, a thin coat of acrylic matte gel medium can be applied to surface of tile and damp-wiped on occasion. These tiles are not meant to be placed in wet areas such as bathrooms or kitchens.

About the Paper

The wall tiles in this project are made with Thai fern paper, which is thick, sturdy, and rustic in appearance. Similar papers are excellent choices in collage and the book arts. Combined with thin papers and text on vellum, Thai botanical papers are popular for invitations; an American cottage industry uses these papers to create custom cards and envelopes.

Tile Tabletop

Make paper tiles to fit a tabletop, right to the edge. Cover with glass or Plexiglas. For a dining table, make tiles that coordinate with different sets of placemats and change them as appropriate.

The papermakers dip their one-piece frame into a large vat of pulp and leave the sheet on the mold to dry in the sun. Village of Bor Sang, northern Thailand.

FOR a successful party, pay attention to every detail. A table set in an unusual way can set the tone for the meal.

This party place setting for an outdoor Asian meal includes a place mat, napkin and napkin ring, place-card holder, fan, rice cracker dish, and an individual lantern for each person. Bamboo chimes, a warm breeze, and gentle music will complete the effect! These pieces are all variations of one simple folded design. They are exceptionally quick and easy to make. Two contrasting papers look best, especially if one is printed.

NEPAL

SUMMER PARTY *place setting*

Materials · *makes four place settings* • 4 sheets 20" x 30" (51 cm x 76 cm) Nepalese printed paper • 2 sheets red paper, 22" x 30" (56 cm x 76 cm) • 2 sheets black paper, 22" x 30" (56 cm x 76 cm) • glue stick • 12 wooden skewers, 10" (25 cm) long • 1 manila file folder • Scotch tape • scissors • metal ruler (to tear against) • pencil • 4 cat food tins (for lantern tea lights) • 4 tea light candles

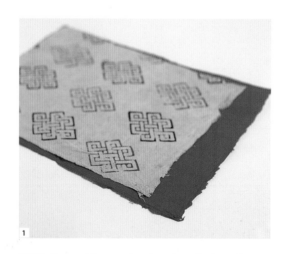

1

STEP 1 Place mat: Tear or cut one large sheet of red paper into quarters. This will be the size of your placemat. Tear one sheet of printed paper into pieces slightly smaller than the printed pieces. Glue the printed paper onto red paper with a glue stick.

Choosing the Paper

Lokta paper is widely available at paper stores and through catalogs. The plain sheets come in a variety of beautiful colors, although these are not lightfast. Some of the patterned papers are printed by women with no other means of income at the Women's Skill Development Project. Many of these charming black and red folk motifs are inspired by traditional textile designs and are popular around the world for collage, the book arts, and wrapping.

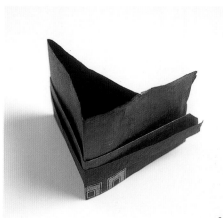

2

3

4

STEP 2 Place-Card Holder: Tear or cut red paper into four pieces, each 9" x 5" (23 cm x 13 cm). Fold in half lengthwise. Fold one long flap in half again. Holding onto the same long flap, fold same side up, allowing top folded edge to show. Divide into thirds, fold, and insert one end into other. Use glue stick to hold in place. Insert name tag into place-card holder. **STEP 3 Napkin Ring:** Tear or cut red paper into four pieces 7 1/2" x 3" (19 cm x 8 cm). Fold as for place-card holder. Divide folded strip into fifths (1 1/2" or 4 cm each). Fold, insert one end into the other, and glue to hold in place. **Napkin:** Tear or cut printed paper into four pieces, 10" (25 cm) square. Fold into quarters. Place in napkin rings. **STEP 4 Lantern:** Tear or cut printed paper into four pieces, 20" x 10" (51 cm x 25 cm). Fold as for place-card holder. Fold into fifths (4" or 10 cm each). Fold one end into other. Glue to hold in place. Place empty cat food tin with tea light inside for illumination.
STEP 5 Rice Cracker Dish: Tear or cut black paper into four pieces, 15" x 10" (38 cm x 25 cm). Fold as for place-card holder. Fold into fifths (3" or 8 cm each). Fold one end into other. Glue to hold in place. Cut top at each corner. Fold down to form dish bottom. Tape closed. **STEP 6 Fan:** Cut manila file folder into four pieces, 5 1/2" x 4" (14 cm x 10 cm). Cut out center to make a 3/4" (2 cm) frame. Tear or cut printed paper into eight pieces, 6" x 5" (15 cm x 13 cm). Glue one piece of file folder to print. Tape three skewers to folder. Glue on another piece of printed paper. Wrap bottom of stick handle with small piece of red paper.

5

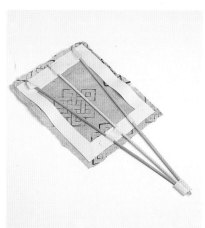

6

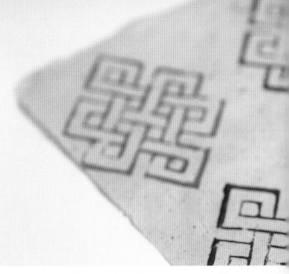

About the Paper

Nepalese handmade paper was imported by Tibetan monks, who kept the paper in large demand until the Chinese occupation of Tibet in 1959. When the Chinese closed the Tibetan borders, Nepalese papermaking virtually ended. Fortunately, papermaking skills were not lost, and during the 1980s, the Nepalese government, the United Nations, and other agencies were able to revive the industry, providing a source of income for people in this desperately poor country. Small Nepalese papermaking companies are now producing beautifully colored sheets of paper as well as stationery, books, and albums.

Asian Centerpiece

Tear or cut one piece of printed paper to 15" x 30" (38 cm x 76 cm). Overlap this with a piece of contrasting colored paper. Fold as for place-card holder. Fold into fifths (6" or 15 cm each). Insert one end into the other. Glue to hold in place. Place fresh, dried, or paper flowers in coffee can inside centerpiece.

Forming a sheet of paper by pouring pulp on a floating mold in a small settlement near Barabise, Nepal, close to the Tibet border.

A HAND-CUT, rustic Mexican bark paper stencil on your wall will be both beautiful and meaningful. To Mexican paper cutters, white amate paper represents Good and is used for offerings, promises, and protections, while brown amate represents Evil and is used to represent spirits, devils, and unfortunate events and to cast spells, cause disease, and create misfortune. Nowadays, amate is also made in a lovely shade of lavender, as was chosen here. A simple white amate cutout design against a pastel wall would be effective too, but brown amate designs should probably be avoided!

LAVENDER WALL *stencil*

Materials · kraft or other inexpensive paper (for practicing) · 1 piece oaktag or thin poster board (for pattern), 18" x 24" (46 cm x 61 cm) · white or lavender amate · white glue or wallpaper paste · scissors · pencil · ruler · tape

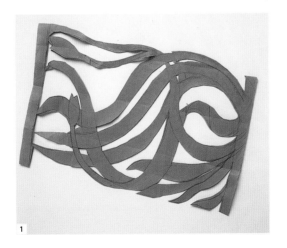

1

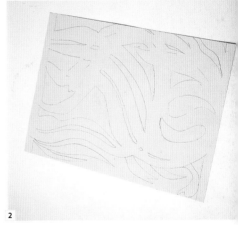

2

TIP
Themes featuring flowers, abstract shapes, leaves, and animals work well for these cutouts. Photographs, wallpaper, and book illustrations can be used for inspiration.

GETTING STARTED Amate sheets measure 23" x 15 ¹/₂" (58 cm x 39 cm). Divide the area to be decorated into units that will use the paper efficiently. Sketch a simple design for the wall. Choose a subject with universal appeal for the frieze that will go around the room. Here, the starting point was a 19th-century Art Nouveau drawing.

STEP 1 Cut a piece of kraft paper to the size that will be used, fold it in half, and adapt the sketch to the paper. Leave a 1" (3 cm) border at top and bottom. Cut out the design, tape to the wall, evaluate, and change as desired. **STEP 2** When the design is finalized on the kraft paper, transfer it to the oaktag or poster board and cut it out. This will become the final pattern.

TIP

Because of the nature of the paper, amate cutout designs are large, chunky, and rough. Do not strive for perfection! And don't worry—all amate cutouts are beautiful.

Treasury of Art Nouveau Design and Ornament, Carol Belanger Grafton, Dover Publications Inc.

4

STEP 3 Fold the amate paper in half. Trace the oaktag pattern onto it. Cut out and unfold as many pieces of amate as are needed to cover the wall area. **STEP 4** Glue the amate cutouts to the wall with wallpaper paste or white glue.

Forming a sheet of amatl, made from the cooked inner bark of the mulberry tree.

About the Paper

Amatl or amate, the traditional Mexican paper used for cutting, is made by pounding mulberry and fig pulp into smooth sheets. This proto-paper was an important part of pre-Columbian rituals. Today, amate is made only by Otimi Indians in the remote village of San Pablito, Puebla State, Mexico. It is sold primarily to tourists, although rural shamans still use it in ceremonies.

Greeting Card Variation

Small amate figures can be cut and glued to ready-made blank cards. These can be sent at any time of year and for any purpose—white for good wishes, brown for bad!

Mexican amatl; this is a cutout of a dark piece of amatl attached to a white sheet.

DELICATE paper lanterns on your table and deck or along an icy walkway can add a twinkling beauty to a memorable evening. These lovely lamps are inexpensively illuminated with tea lights. By using two layers of handmade paper, one translucent and one opaque, and imaginative cutout shapes, you can make lanterns for any occasion from the Fourth of July to the winter solstice—snowflakes, anyone?

To make lanterns that rest on tabletops and decks, use 10" (25 cm) skewers; use longer skewers to make lanterns with feet that can be securely planted in sand or snow.

PHILIPPINES

SAND *and* SNOW *lantern*

Materials · 1 sheet opaque paper for outer layer, 12" x 19" (30 cm x 48 cm) · 1 rectangle thin cardboard, 6" x 10" (15 cm x 25 cm) · 1 sheet transluscent paper for inner layer, 10" x 18" (25 cm x 46 cm) · 2 strips thick paper, 1" x 18" (3 cm x 46 cm) · 6 strips of oaktag, 1" x 6" (3 cm x 15 cm) · 3 wooden barbecue skewers, 10" (25 cm) or 12" (30 cm) long · Scotch tape · pencil · ruler · craft knife with sharp #11 blade · white glue · waxed paper · 2" (5 cm) brush · scrap paper · cutting mat

TIP
For illumination, set a tea light in an empty cat food can and place inside lantern.

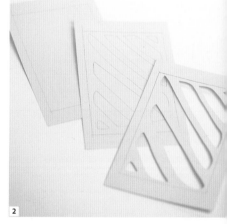

STEP 1 Fold in 1" (3 cm) top hem and 1" (3 cm) bottom hem on outer paper. Fold in 1" (3 cm) hem on one short side. Fold into three panels, 6" x 10" (15 cm x 25 cm) each panel. Place one wooden skewer in each vertical fold. Tape skewers to paper on top and bottom. **STEP 2** Cut a 6" x 10" (15 cm x 25 cm) thin cardboard rectangle. This is the finished size of one panel of the lantern. Draw a pencil line 1/3" (1 cm) in from the vertical edges and 1" (3 cm) in from the top and bottom. Draw freehand shapes (not too large) on the thin cardboard rectangle and cut out with knife on cardboard or cutting mat. Simple curves or straight lines work best. Cut out shapes to create stencil.

Choosing the Paper

Sand and Snow Lanterns look best if the outer layer of paper is darker in color than the inner layer; both are particularly effective if they have texture or inclusions (such as unryu and lace papers from Japan or botanical papers from India) that will show when illuminated. It's possible, however, to make spectacular lanterns with materials close at hand. For example, use brown grocery bags and paper doilies to produce a rustic look on a wood deck, or combine freezer wrap and colored tissue for a festive party atmosphere on winter snow.

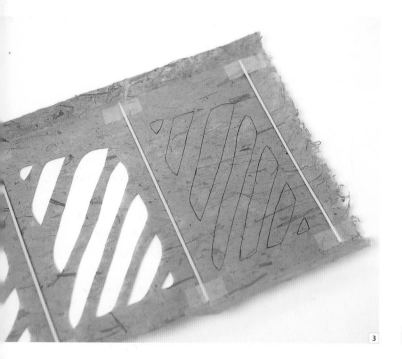

3

4

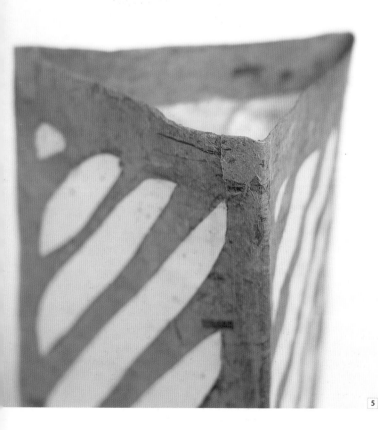

5

STEP 3 Use the thin cardboard stencil to trace a pattern of shapes onto each panel of lantern outer paper. Cut out shapes. **STEP 4** To prevent paper from sticking to work surface, place outer paper on waxed paper, folded side up. Coat with white glue. Throw away waxed paper. Then place on clean scrap paper. Place inner paper on outer paper. Rub. Glue on two strips of thick paper or thin cardboard at top and bottom edges. Fold over hem of outer paper onto strips. **STEP 5** This step should be done while the papers are wet with glue so that the lantern dries into its final position. Crease folds of paper into a triangular shape. Stand lantern on edges. Glue end tab (created by the overlap of the outer paper) onto the outside surface of the opposite end of the outer paper.

TIP

Consider using file folders for the lantern panels. Readily at hand and just stiff enough to stand, file folders are an ingenious substitute for thin cardboard.

About the Paper

The outer layer of the Sand and Snow Lantern is blue abaca paper from the Philippines with pieces of chopped bamboo added. Of the more than thirty different fibers indigenous to the Philippines that can be used to make paper, the most common is abaca, sometimes called Manila hemp. The whole plant is harvested and produces a long-fiber pulp that can make either thin or thick strong sheets. The West is perhaps most familiar with abaca as the material for tea bags.

The inner layer of the Sand and Snow Lantern is a type of chiri (meaning bits of bark) paper that was made in Taiwan as an imitation of Japanese paper made from kozo, a long fiber plant. In its finest form, kozo paper is thin, pure, and white; in this example, chiri remain in the pulp for decorative effect.

Looking at a grove of *Musa textilis*, a plant in the banana family. The fiber is called abaca and is used to make rope (Manila hemp) and paper.

IMPROVISE

Achieve an altogether different shape by loosely wrapping the lantern paper around an oatmeal container. This will produce a cylindrical lantern that just fits around a cat food can and tea light. Or, instead of cutting the shapes completely out of the outer layer, consider leaving them partially attached and folding them up, down, or sideways. The candlelight will cause these "flaps" to create fascinating, dramatic shadows.

Paper House

Newspapers and magazines make surprisingly sturdy construction materials—witness the Paper House in Rockport, Massachusetts. Long before recycling was an environmental issue, Elis F. Stenman invented a way to build his summer house out of newspapers—over 100,000 of them. Each page was rolled to look like a stick of bamboo, cut to the appropriate size, nailed or glued together, and varnished. The walls, roof, fireplace mantle, lamps, chairs, and even a piano were made of newspapers, and colorful braided newspaper curtains were hung in the windows.

It took almost 20 years to make the Paper House, but it still stands, a testimony to the strength of its material.

COMPARED to the Paper House, the table presented here is a tiny effort. It is made of rolled pages from the New Yorker as a modest tribute to this famous American periodical's 75th anniversary. This small stand can be used as a table for a small planter (made from a recycled ice cream container) or for a notepad and pencils. The technique can be carried much further. Long-time subscribers who have saved old issues could perhaps make their own New Yorker country house!

USA

NEW YORKER table

Materials · about 12 square feet corrugated cardboard (from old boxes) · 6–8 issues of the *New Yorker* · 2 cardboard paper towel tubes · white glue · brush for glue · glue gun · 2 bags glue gun sticks · scissors · knife

GETTING STARTED Make the tabletop by cutting 10–16 pieces of corrugated cardboard (this number depends on the thickness of the cardboard) the size of a *New Yorker* cover. Glue these together into a stack with a glue gun.

1

2

3

4

STEP 1 Cut two pieces of cardboard the size of half the magazine cover (horizontally). Glue these together with a glue gun and attach to the bottom of the tabletop, right in the middle with a border of approximately 1" (3 cm). **STEP 2** Measure two paper towel tubes against the short dimension of the tabletop and trim to this measurement. Cut the pages of one issue of the *New Yorker* the same length as each tube. Roll and stuff into the tubes. Cover the outside of the tubes by gluing a page around them with white glue. **STEP 3** Roll 60 *New Yorker* pages into thin tubes and glue the edges closed. Glue these tubes onto sides, top, and edges of the cardboard underneath the tabletop. **STEP 4** Glue the covered tubes to the bottom of the tabletop with a glue gun. Glue a *New Yorker* cover to the bottom of the tabletop with white glue.

TIP
For visual interest, make sure headlines are readable when glued.

paper recycling in the USA

The first paper made in America (in 1690) was composed entirely of recycled materials—cotton and linen rags. Unfortunately, by the 19th century, rags were scarce and new materials for producing paper were needed. Since then, wood pulp has become the dominant pulp material, with the result that forests have been ravaged and waters polluted in the papermaking process.

As the largest producer, consumer, and waster of paper in the world, most people agree that the United States has a responsibility to take the lead in creating efficient and profitable ways to recycle paper. Some large paper mills are doing this as are some small mills and American hand papermakers. Individual consumers may not be able to build a house like Mr. Stenman's in Massachusetts (see Paper House, pg. 50), but creative recycling solutions at home, in schools, and at work all help to reduce paper waste.

Today, a small number of American paper mills are using recycled materials for machine-made papers. One company, Green Fields of San Diego, California, is attempting to produce, on a commercial scale, a handmade paper that uses recycled materials. This company makes large sheets, note cards, and stationery out of recycled pulp with junk mail inclusions. Sometimes the words are still visible—a kind of poetry for a throwaway society!

You can recycle your own wastepaper by making Junk Mail sheets. Follow the instructions in the back of this book (see pg. 96), using recycled paper for the pulp. Sprinkle cut or torn pieces of junk mail into the pulp, and the result will be a strong, colorful, amusing paper that can be used for many purposes, including projects in this book. Pictured here are a placemat, a journal, and an invitation. Instructions for similar items can be found in other chapters.

COMMERCIALLY produced books of affirmations are everywhere these days, but a handmade book containing affirmations you choose yourself is one of a kind. This highly personal project takes its cue from the traditional Tibetan prayer book. Its form is long and narrow, with a post or cord passing through a hole in the pages. As pages are read, they are moved along the post and turned over onto a neat pile.

This book form may seem unusual to Westerners, but it is remarkably adaptable and offers opportunities to make beautiful and personally meaningful objects. In the example here, a new affirmation is revealed as each page is turned.

TIBET

TIBETAN PRAYER *book*

Materials · 8 sheets good-quality paper or vellum, 8 1/2" x 11" (22 cm x 28 cm) · 8 sheets natural-colored lokta for pages, 18" x 26" (46 cm x 66 cm) · 1 sheet contrasting colored lokta for cover · 1 sheet woodblock-printed lokta for cover design · 18" x 24" (46 cm x 61 cm) book board · 1 piece oaktag or thick paper, 12" x 18" (30 cm x 46 cm) · 1 package notebook ring reinforcements · white glue · 4" (1.2 m) thick cord · pencil · ruler · scissors · utility knife · hole punch · needle · thread · electric drill or awl

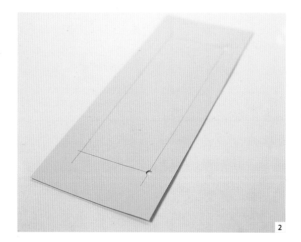

GETTING STARTED Print the affirmations or other text (quotations, prayers, etc.) in a beautiful calligraphic hand on pieces of good-quality paper or vellum 8 1/2" x 2 3/4" (22 cm x 8 cm) in size. Four sayings fit onto one sheet of 8 1/2" x 11" (22 cm x 28 cm) paper. Alternatively, print these on a computer.

STEP 1 To make the pages of the book, tear the natural lokta paper into eighths. Each page should measure 5" x 13" (13 cm x 33 cm). Make two lokta pages for each affirmation. **STEP 2** On a piece of oaktag the same size as the pages, draw lines 2" (5 cm) in from the short edges and 1" (3 cm) in from the long edges. Holding the paper horizontally, punch a hole at the top two intersections of these lines. Use this template to mark the holes on the pages. Stick a reinforcement on each spot. Glue two pages together, rough side out and reinforcements inside.

3

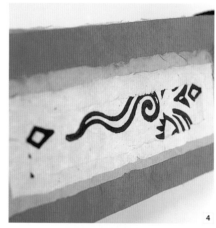

4

STEP 3 To make the book cover, cut six pieces of book board the same size as the pages. Glue together in threes to make front and back covers. Cut two pieces of colored lokta paper 1" (3 cm) larger than the covers and glue them on. Cut off corners, turn in, and glue on (see How to Make Corners, pg.14). Line inside with another color. **STEP 4** Use scraps of the colored lokta paper and a piece of woodblock- printed paper to create a simple collage on the front of the book. **STEP 5** Use the template (from step 2) as a guide to drill holes through the stack of assembled covers and pages. Pass a cord through the holes, knot at the ends, and tie to secure.

5

Serene Meditation Collage

Create a meditation piece by using similar papers and creating a simple collage.

The printing room of a Tibetan monastery, where hand printing is being done.

About the Paper

For centuries, Tibetans produced lokta, or daphne paper, which provides a strong surface for embellished script and illustration. The craft declined for many reasons, but Paper Road/Tibet, a nonprofit organization in Washington, D.C., is working to revitalize it, teaching the skill to students in Lhasa, the capital, and helping market their products.

Lokta paper is also made by exiles in Kathmandu, Nepal, who produce books, journals, and stationery. Their organization works with Paper Road/Tibet and donates a portion of its profits to promote sustainable lokta fiber harvesting.

Examining the plant used in traditional Tibetan papermaking. The plant is *Stellera chamaejasme*. It is the root of the plant that contains the fiber. The root is woody and can measure more than two inches in diameter and twenty inches in length, making it very difficult to dig up in the rocky soil of Tibet.

Collage by Gail Hercher

PAPYRUS is a fascinating material to use for lampshades; the overlapping strips that make up each sheet are clearly visible in the light. Further, although it appears brittle, papyrus is actually quite strong and supple, especially when wet with glue. Finally, considering the labor involved in making it, papyrus is remarkably inexpensive.

To develop an Egyptian design for your lampshade, look at books in the library. In this example, the wedja, the Egyptian symbol for "eye of Horus," was used as inspiration. This symbol means "to be whole" and is an Egyptian charm for healing.

EGYPT

PAPYRUS *lampshade*

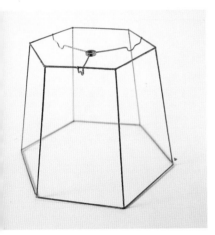

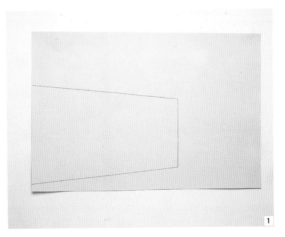

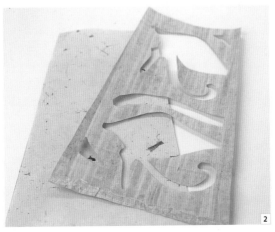

Materials • 1 piece oaktag or thick paper, 18" x 24" (46 cm x 61 cm) • 1 faceted lampshade frame and matching base • 3–4 pieces papyrus, 11" x 17" each (28 cm x 43 cm) • 1 sheet paper to line shade, 22" x 30" (56 cm x 76 cm) • scrap paper • white glue and brush • extra-tacky white glue with small nozzle tip • spring clothespins • scissors • knife • cutting board • pencil

GETTING STARTED To make the lampshade pattern, trace one lampshade facet (panel) onto oaktag or thick paper. This pattern should extend beyond the top and bottom of the shade by 1/2" (1 cm) and the metal frame sides by about 1" (3 cm).

STEP 1 Using the prepared pattern, cut six pieces of papyrus and six liners. **STEP 2** Using images from books on Egypt as inspiration, draw a design on the panel pattern that is interesting but also easy to cut. The design can be an allover pattern (as in the example shown here) or a frieze on the bottom and top of the shade.

TIP
It's easier to match a shade to a base than the other way around.

TIPS

If the lampshade frame comes from a yard sale, clean the shade and remove any previous covering. Make sure that the wiring in the base is safe. Take it to a hardware store if you are uncertain.

Take advantage of copiers to enlarge or reduce images to suit your purpose.

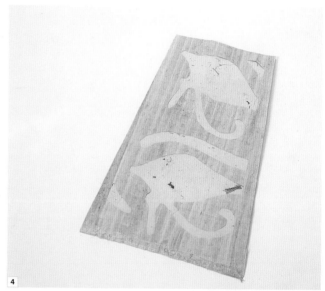

STEP 3 Cut the design out of the pattern to obtain a pattern/stencil combination. Trace it onto the six panels of papyrus. Cut the design out of each panel. **STEP 4** Brush each piece of papyrus with white glue and stick it to the liner paper. Rub with clean scrap paper to make the papyrus lie smoothly. **STEP 5** To attach the shade, spread tacky glue from a container with a small nozzle onto the lampshade frame. Lay the lined papyrus panel on top, fold top and bottom ¹/₂" (1 cm) over the frame, and secure with spring clothespins. Trim panel sides to edges of frame. Proceed facet by facet around the lampshade. Each papyrus facet will overlap the next.

Cutout Papyrus Lampshade

Because papyrus sheets are small, it's impossible to make a large shade in one piece. As an easy option, glue cutout papyrus shapes onto a large lampshade surface. The result will be as interesting as the smaller shades.

About the Paper

Papyrus, a proto-paper, is made from the pith of the papyrus plant, which is triangular in cross section. The plant is peeled, sliced into thin strips, and soaked in water. Sheets are formed by overlapping the strips at right angles and pressing them until dry.

Papyrus was an important commodity in ancient Egypt and, after the Roman conquest in 30 B.C., the chief writing material of the Graeco-Roman world for almost 1,000 years.

Papyrus Travel Journal

Create a travel journal using papyrus to cover the book. The papyrus becomes soft and flexible when wet, making it easy to cover the book with smooth finished edges. The unique texture and transparency of the papyrus will make this travel journal a favorite memoir or gift to someone special.

Making a papyrus sheet in Cairo, Egypt.

THE travel journal is an absolute necessity for recording adventures and trips to exotic places—a place to keep notes, sketches, and photos. This project is easy because the materials are available almost everywhere—a file folder, a paper bag, 8 ½" x 11" (22 cm x 28 cm) paper, needle, thread, and a label from a tin can. The journals presented here, which use three Costa Rican papers, are sturdy and will travel well. Use them, for example, to record visits to coffee, cigar, and banana plantations. Afterward, enjoy reading them over and looking at sketches of the rain forest while sitting next to a cozy fire at home. Or, if your journeys keep you closer to home, jot down your garden notes, to-do list, or use as a daily journal.

COSTA RICA

PLANTATION PAPER
travel journal

Materials · 37 sheets 8 ½" x 11" (22 cm x 28 cm) paper · 1 manila file folder · 1 brown grocery bag · 1 tin can label · white glue · glue brush · thread or twine · awl · scissors · needle

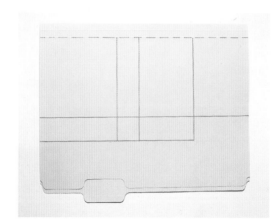

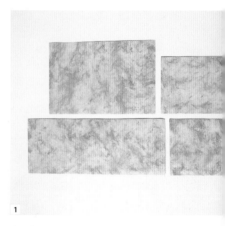

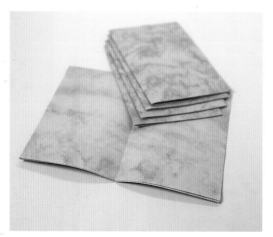

GETTING STARTED The materials and equipment listed here can make four different journals. The size (and shape) of each is determined by the size to which the file folder is cut (see diagram for options). First cut the file folder, using the diagram to measure the front cover of the journal. Fold along the creases at the bottom of the folder to create the 1" (3 cm) spine of the book. The opposite side of the folder will be the back cover. Then cut or tear interior page paper to size to fit folder (see diagram).

STEP 1 Choose a size for your travel journal by referring to the diagram. (There are four options.) Prepare 37 interior sheets of paper to size. Nest 35 of them into five signatures, or packets, of seven pages each. Save the other two sheets.

2

TIP
Sometimes brown grocery bags sport interesting designs or print. If yours does, you may want to make this the outside of the cover.

3

4

STEP 2 The manila folder will be the inside cover of the book. Cut it to the size required (see diagram). Fold it on the middle lines to form the spine. Put the pages into the manila folder; they should fit perfectly. **STEP 3** Open a large brown grocery bag by cutting down seam and cutting off bottom. Smooth it flat. Place prepared folder/cover on bag and cut bag 1 ¹/₂" (4 cm) larger than cover all around. **STEP 4** Spread white glue on the back of the bag. Lay on folder cover and rub flat. Cut off corners of bag close to folder and fold in sides, making corners as perfect as possible (see How to Make Corners, pg. 14).

STEP 5 Line the inside of the cover with the two reserved pages. Overlap them at the spine only. Glue the tin can label onto the cover to distinguish front from back.

5

TIP

Instructions are provided here for a bookbinding technique called the longstitch. Once you have learned this pattern, you can easily change it to create your own version.

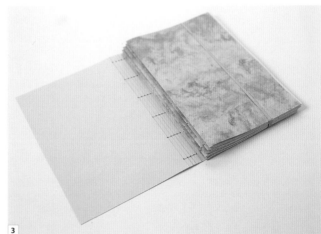

LONGSTITCH *binding*

STEP 1 Measure in ½" (1 cm) from head of spine and draw a line horizontally across spine. Repeat this at bottom of spine. Divide spine area within these two lines into five equal units and draw horizontal lines at these points. There will be a total of six horizontal lines across spine. **STEP 2** Divide spine vertically into five parts and draw lines the complete length of the book to show these divisions. Punch a series of 30 holes with small awl point where vertical lines cross horizontal lines. **STEP 3** Position neatly stacked pile of 5 signatures next to cover, so that the spine and folded edges of the papers face you. Place a dot on each fold of the paper to align with each hole in the spine. This will clearly delineate where the stitching will be placed for each nest of papers. Punch holes with awl through each nest of paper. **STEP 4** Using strong thread, begin stitching on the outside of the first signature (see diagram) until it is attached. Add the second signature and sew as the first. Continue to add signatures until all are sewn in. Tie knots to secure.

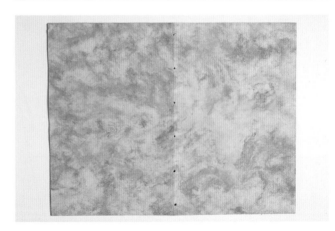

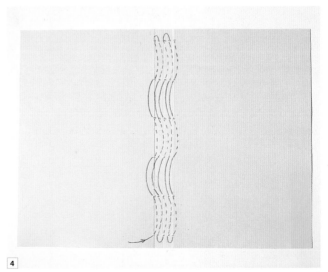

About the Paper

The Costa Rica Natural Company makes papers that combine postconsumer paper waste with agricultural byproducts from local plantations. Banana, coffee, and tobacco waste fibers are prepared by Earth College students in Costa Rica, processed into paper in El Salvador, and returned for conversion into notepads, stationery, journals, and sketchpads that are marketed globally. A percentage of each sale goes to an Earth College scholarship fund.

The lush Costa Rican mountainside and fertile lands provide the ideal environment for banana, coffee, and tobacco plantations.

Experiment

Create travel journals of various sizes, and use them for travel and daily activities. Once you are familiar with the longstitch binding, experiment with other types of bindings.

THIS tiny purse was inspired by a Korean pouch housed at the Peabody Essex Museum in Salem, Massachusetts. The original, made of thick black hanji paper folded origami-style into a pouch for tobacco and tinder, is secured by a silk cord running through a bat-shaped metal clasp. In this version, the folding has been simplified and a Velcro dot and vintage button are used for the closure. The paper is painted with inks, layered, sewn on a machine for strength, buffed with petroleum jelly for flexibility and protection, and folded into the perfect container for a credit card and some cash!

KOREA
EXOTIC EVENING *purse*

Materials · 1 sheet hanji paper, 24" x 36" (61 cm x 91 cm) • black india ink • red india ink • thread • needle (for hand sewing) or sewing machine • Velcro dot • vintage button • ruler • pencil • scissors • petroleum jelly

TIP
Thick kozo paper can be substituted for the hanji paper.

GETTING STARTED Cut or tear the paper into quarters, 12" x 18" (30 cm x 46 cm). Crumple each quarter into a ball to thoroughly wrinkle. Flatten each piece of paper.

STEP 1 Paint two pieces of flattened paper with black ink and two with red. Let dry. **STEP 2** Place the two red sheets of paper together, and sew in a random pattern to create an interesting design. Repeat with the two pieces of black paper.

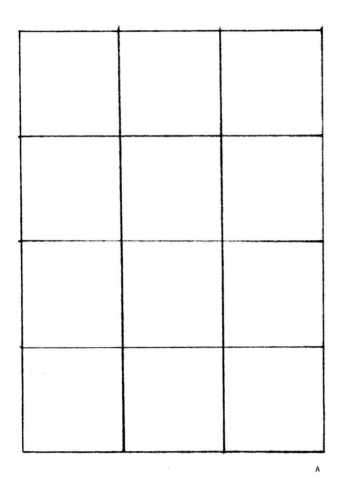

A

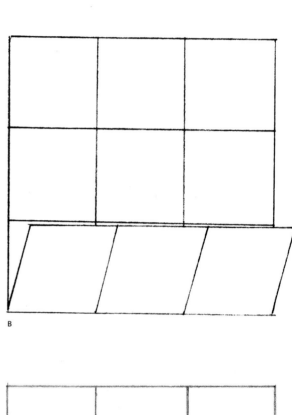

B

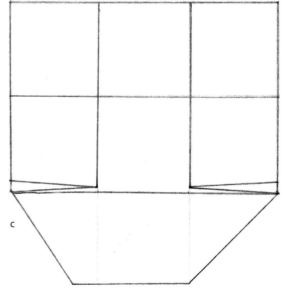

C

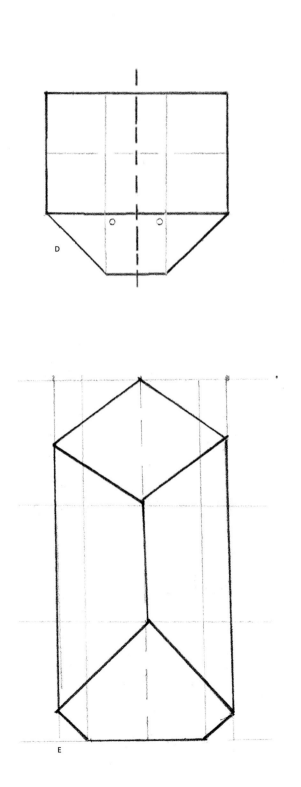

D

E

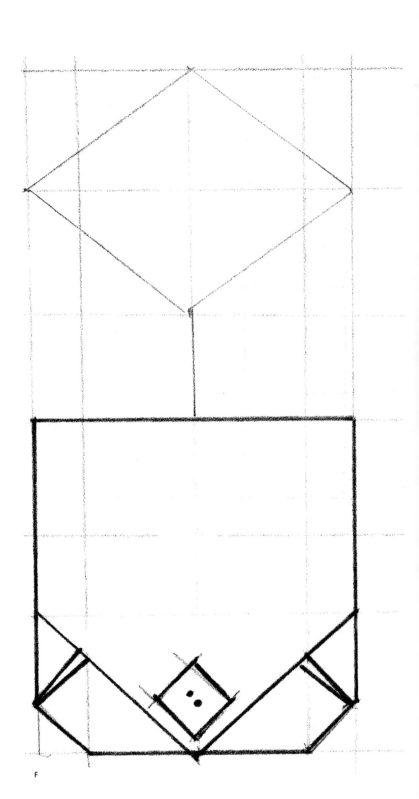

F

3

STEP 3 Put the red and black pieces together and sew on three sides. Turn so that the seam is inside (like a pillowcase). Turn under a $\frac{1}{2}$" (1 cm) seam allowance on the open end and sew closed. The sewn rectangle of paper should measure approximately 11" x 17" (28 cm x 43 cm) and be black on one side, red on the other. **STEP 4** Red side up, fold the rectangle into a purse, following diagram. Sew two small buttons as shown in diagram. Sew on the vintage button and attach the Velcro dot to the flap.

4

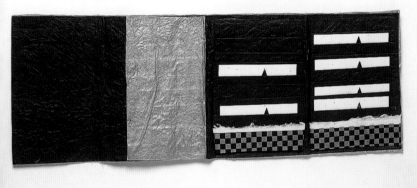

About the Paper

Koreans, like the Japanese, have traditionally used the mulberry plant (tak) to make hanji paper for books, painting, calligraphy, chests, and baskets, but they are especially well known for applying it to floors where it was laminated, oiled to a warm honey color, and heated with pipes underneath. Like the Japanese, Koreans have also substituted paper for cloth (even weatherproofing it to make rain gear) and leather as in the Korean tobacco pouch that inspired the design for this small evening purse.

Making a sheet of paper on a Korean mold. Note that the mold is vertical in design and is dipped from side to side to form the sheet.

Business Card Holder

An elegant business card holder is easily made by folding a sheet of paper in half to create a long rectangle. Fold the paper horizontally into fourths. Glue a pleated sheet inside to accommodate the business cards inside. Fold outside paper into quarters and wrap around itself. Close with a button and Velcro dot.

A THREE-PANEL folding frame is a lovely way to display photographs. This project makes a true heirloom. Don't forget to sign it! Fine Dutch linen bookcloth, used to cover the frame, offers solid protection over the acid-free mat board base. The paste papers are made with Ingres Fabriano, a machine-made rag paper from the oldest paper mill in Europe. European paste papers originally served as endpapers for books and featured small, regular patterns. Today, however, paste papers are an art form in their own right, offering artists an uninhibited way to make luscious patterns on a paper surface.

ITALY

THREE-PANEL *frame*

Materials · *for 5" x 5" (13 cm x 13 cm) photographs* · 3 pieces acid-free mat board, 9" x 9" (23 cm x 23 cm) · 3 pieces light-weight cardboard or posterboard, 8 3/4" x 8 3/4" (22 cm x 22 cm), with 5" x 5" (13 cm x 13 cm) opening cut in the center (these are the mats) · white glue · YES paste · wheat paste · 2 pieces Ingres Fabriano cream paper, 19" x 26" (48 cm x 66 cm) · acrylic paint in burnt umber, white, silver · 1 linear foot natural linen book cloth · masking tape · pencil · ruler · utility knife · brushes and containers for glues and paint · plastic plaster comb from hardware store · bone folder

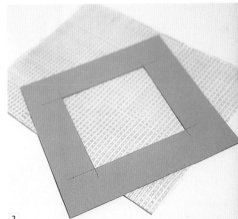

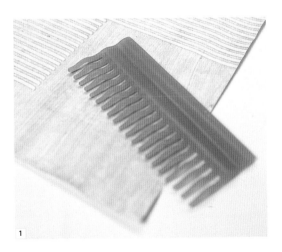

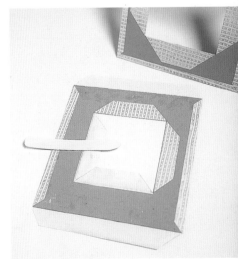

GETTING STARTED This project employs three glues, each for a different purpose: white glue for the book cloth (which is protected from wetness by a tissue lining), YES paste to glue down the paste papers (so that they don't warp and wrinkle), and wheat paste, which is mixed with paint to produce the correct consistency for combing.

STEP 1 To make paste paper, mix one cup water and about three tablespoons wheat paste. Add about one tablespoon white paint, one teaspoon burnt umber paint, and two tablespoons silver paint. Mix well. Brush this mixture onto the Fabriano paper. Comb through the paint with the plaster comb, making a small-scale design. Set aside to dry. Don't worry if the paper curls. **STEP 2** Cut pieces of paste paper 1" (3 cm) larger than the three pieces of thin board. These will be the mats for the photographs. Glue a paste paper to each mat. Cut off corners and turn in sides. Make an "X" in the center of each of the three mats and fold paper edges to the inside.

TIP
To make lump-free wheat paste, sprinkle dry powder slowly into cold water at whip speed in a blender.

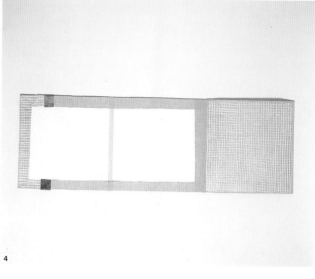

3   4

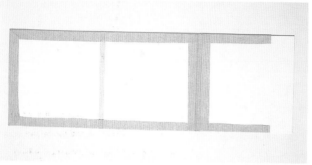

STEP 3 Tape photograph to the back of the mat. **STEP 4** Lay the three pieces of mat board in a horizontal line on the book cloth with ½" (1 cm) between the first and second pieces and ¼" (.5 cm) between the second and third pieces. Cut out book cloth 1" (3 cm) larger around mat board pieces but 2" (5 cm) in from the leading edge of the first piece of mat board. **STEP 5** Spread glue onto book cloth and lay down pieces of mat board. Cut corners off at a 45-degree angle and turn over edges. Glue 2" x 9" (5 cm x 23 cm) pieces of book cloth over the spines, and rub the grooves with a bone folder. Glue a piece of matching paste paper to the front of the triptych. Weight and dry overnight. **STEP 6** Glue a photo frame unit to each section of the mat board on the book cloth. Place weights on top and dry overnight.

5

6

TIP
To protect your photograph, attach a piece of acetate, 8" x 8" (20 x 20 cm), to the back of the mat. Then attach the photo.

Wall Art

Scraps of paste papers can be framed as art for the wall. Replace the traditional small-scale pattern with wide, free brushstrokes and randomly combed designs.

Art by Gail Hercher

About the Paper

Founded in 1276, the Fabriano paper mill is the oldest in Europe and produces fine handmade, mold-made, and machine-made papers. Fabriano artisans, who served Michelangelo, Leonardo, and Van Eyck in their day, invented the watermark, a symbol of high-quality paper.

The town of Fabriano is in a hilly area of clear air and pure water, ideal for papermaking. The mill uses raw cotton and pollutes so little that Sunday fishermen even fish downstream!

This image of the Fabriano Mill, dated 1450, shows workers stirring pulp, sheet forming at the vat, couching sheets, pressing , and restacking sheets.

BRIAN THOMAS, an artist from Salem, Massachusetts, developed an unusual use for wasp nests—to fashion beautiful baskets. (The paperlike wasp nest gave French naturalist René-Antoine Ferchault de Réamur (1683–1757) the idea to use wood for making paper. His research eventually led to the first viable papermaking machine to rely on wood pulp.)

Brian substitutes paper bags when wasp nests are unavailable. Here, a brown grocery bag is used for the exterior of the basket and strong handmade Bhutanese paper for the interior. Ordinary cardboard is shaped into a base onto which these two materials are glued. The result is exceedingly sturdy but not waterproof.

BHUTAN

TEXTURED *bowl*

Materials · 2 pieces cardboard, about 12" x 12" (30 cm x 30 cm) · brown paper bag or kraft paper torn into pieces about 1" x 3" (3 cm x 8 cm) · Bhutanese paper torn into pieces about 1" x 3" (3 cm x 8 cm) · reed or vine about 2' (61 cm) long · synthetic sinew or strong thread · white glue · scissors · sanding paper · knife · clips · needle · awl

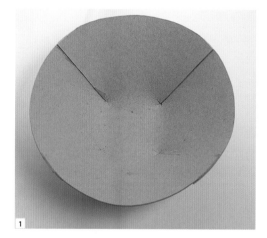 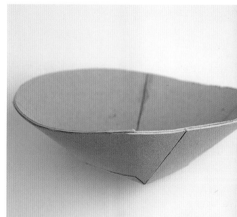

GETTING STARTED Find a thin vine to edge the bowl. Brian usually uses bittersweet. Its berries are poisonous, so clean the vine before bringing it indoors.

STEP 1 Cut in about 3" (8 cm) from each corner of the cardboard toward the center. Overlap sides to form an angled bowl. Fill in spaces with extra triangles of cardboard. Make a second bowl and glue it inside the first. Trim edges and sand, if necessary, to create seamless appearance.

TIP
To create a variety of bowls, experiment with size and shape by using a manila file folder. The goal is to discover visually pleasing proportions that will also make a useful basket. Use the best folder shape as a pattern for the cardboard.

STEP 2 Using pieces of paper bag and glue, cover both sides of bowl with three layers of paper. Pay particular attention to the outside; create a pattern, if desired, with tones of brown ink on paper bag. Let dry.

2

3 4

STEP 3 Glue two to three layers of Bhutanese paper to inside of bowl; smooth with fingers so that the edges do not show. Let dry. **STEP 4** Prepare a vine for the edge of the bowl. It can be stripped of bark or used as is for rustic effect. Size it to the bowl and clip into a curve. Put aside for later use.

5 6

STEP 5 With an awl or very fine electric drill bit, make holes about $^1/4$" (.5 cm) from edge and $^1/4$" (.5 cm) from each other around bowl. Precise placement of these holes is important, as careful stitching will provide an interesting contrast to the rustic surfaces of the bowl. **STEP 6** Whipstitch the vine to the edge of the bowl using synthetic sinew or strong thread.

TIP
Paper bowls can be painted with matte acrylic gel for protection and damp-wiped for dust. They cannot be used to hold liquids or other moist foods.

About the Paper

Any combination of papers can be used for this bowl because its structure and strength are formed with the cardboard and papier-mâché layers. Thus, texture and color can be used for different effects: a dark, crinkled exterior and pastel interior is chic, a bark exterior and papyrus interior rustic, a floral exterior and sheer interior delicate.

Rectangular Basket

A cardboard base form can be made into almost any simple shape and covered with decorative and handmade papers. Here, a rectangle is made into a footed tray and whipstitched with raffia.

The papermaker is showing his screen and wood frame that he uses for papermaking. The paper is formed in a fairly shallow vat. Village of Nobding in central Bhutan.

A WOVEN basket is the perfect combination of practical and beautiful—it is strong enough to hold the sundry objects that clutter a home, yet can be displayed on a bookshelf or small table. Woven with sturdy Japanese kozo paper painted with ink, this small basket can hold everything from pencils, photos, mail, or receipts to craft supplies. The kozo used to make this basket can usually be found in art supply stores on a roll, as it is used for calligraphy and accepts inks readily. Other types of kozo, sold by the sheet, will also work but will probably be more expensive.

WOVEN KOZO *basket*

Materials · kozo paper, on a roll or in sheets—enough to make 17 strips 20" (51 cm) long and 2" (5 cm) wide (16 for basket, 1 for rim) · bottled inks, preferably lightfast (refer to information on bottle), 2 or 3 colors in the same color family · small plastic containers, preferably with lids, one for each color of ink · water · metal ruler · scissors · spring clothespins · 2" (5 cm) wide paintbrushes · glue stick · thread for rim sewing

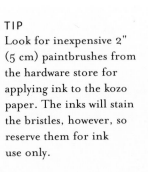

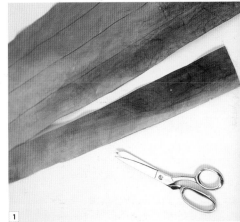

TIP
Look for inexpensive 2" (5 cm) paintbrushes from the hardware store for applying ink to the kozo paper. The inks will stain the bristles, however, so reserve them for ink use only.

GETTING STARTED Lay the kozo paper flat on a table. Protect the work surface with newspaper or plastic. Pour ink into plastic containers and dilute with water until the desired tint is achieved. Test on a small piece of kozo; the inks dry lighter than they first appear. Have fun painting the inks onto the kozo! Mistakes are impossible because the paper will be cut into strips.

STEP 1 When the inked papers are dry, cut with scissors or tear against metal ruler into 17 strips, 20" x 2" (51 cm x 5 cm). Put one strip aside for the rim. Fold each strip into quarters lengthwise. Fold one quarter of each strip lengthwise toward the center and then each half again to produce a long strip with folded edges on each side. Closely arrange eight folded strips on a table and weave the other eight across them. Tighten as much as possible and clip with clothespins at the corners. This is the bottom of the basket.

STEP 2 Find the two center strips on a side, cross one over the other, and clip with a clothespin. Repeat on each side. These four overlaps should form an angle; they will be the bottom corners of the finished basket. Marking them with erasable ink or a string will help with orientation while weaving. **STEP 3** When the corners are formed in step 2, the center strips automatically point in the right direction for weaving the sides of the basket. Weave using the basic under-over pattern, clipping with clothespins to hold the basket together. This process may seem cumbersome at first, but after a few rows the basket will start to hold together. At this stage, don't worry about tension—just keep going.

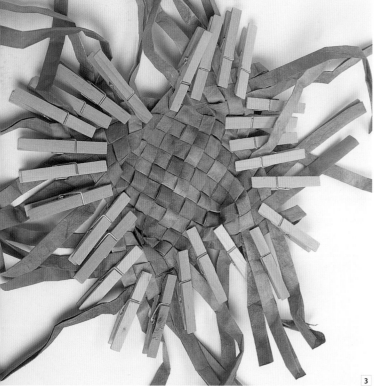

The basket is well woven if you don't see any holes when
you hold it up to a light.

4

STEP 4 Continue weaving until the basket achieves the desired height (or you run
out of paper). Gradually tighten one strip at a time, aiming for even tension
throughout the basket. Trim the top strips evenly, using a glue stick to glue them
together. This will prevent the basket from falling apart as the rim is applied.

5

STEP 5 Take the strip of paper that was held aside. Fold over the top edge of the basket and glue it into place with a 1" (3 cm) overlap. Use carpet thread, waxed linen, raffia, or another suitable material to blanket-stitch or whipstitch over the top edge.

About the Paper

Of the three traditional fibers used in Japan for papermaking, kozo is the toughest, retaining its strength even when crumpled or folded. Sometimes called paper mulberry, kozo ranges in texture from fine to coarse and in color from pure white to tan. One variety, hon-mino-gami, is designated an Important Intangible Cultural Property and is made only by the family that developed it.

Experiment

Weave a variety of sizes of baskets using different lengths and quantities of kozo paper strips. Experiment with different colors, or use kozo paper in its natural form to create a serene, cream-colored basket.

Sheets of finished paper are dried on boards in the town of Ogawa, Japan.

PAPER shoes and slippers offer an opportunity to wear something that is totally outrageous, yet inexpensive. The example here uses a recycled corrugated cardboard carton, tree-wound paper tape (from the hardware store), joss paper (from Chinatown), and decorative paper. If joss paper is unavailable, simply use other decorative papers. If you want a conversation starter, this is it; no one can resist asking about these shoes. Paper shoes and slippers can be worn once or twice—after that, they make great bookends. You can also make them to match your wallpaper or get really carried away and coordinate with the Party Place Setting (see pg. 38).

CHINA

DELICATE CHINESE *slippers*

Materials · 1 large corrugated cardboard carton (smooth surface on both sides) · exposed (ridged) corrugated cardboard (this material can sometimes be found in cases of wine) · white glue · tree-wound tape · decorative paper · decorative embellishments · joss paper · utility knife · pencil · scissors · small clamp

GETTING STARTED Make a sole pattern by standing on a piece of smooth cardboard in bare feet. Trace about ¼" (.5 cm) beyond your foot. Cut out this pattern. By flipping it over, you can use it for both the right and the left foot.

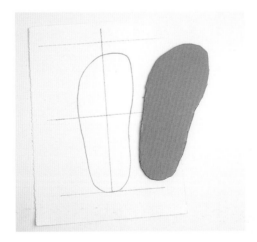

STEP 1 Decide how high to make the base of the slipper. Cut out enough soles for about half this height. Cut an equal number of heels using the heel part of the pattern only. Important: The corrugations must go across the sole, not along its length.

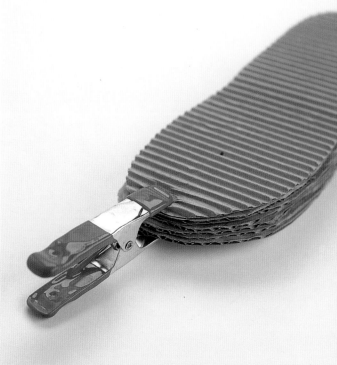

STEP 2 Set top sole aside for use in making slipper top. Glue soles and heels together, alternating them, with white glue. Cut bottom treads out of the ridged corrugated paper for better traction. Glue the cardboard onto bottoms of slippers. Use the clamp to hold together while glue dries.

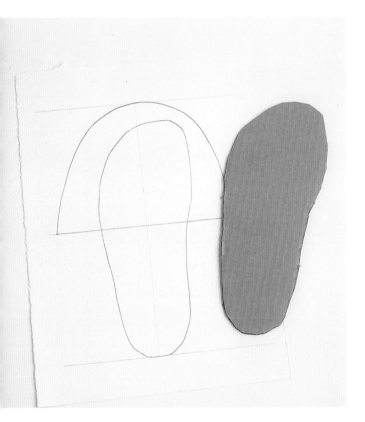

3

STEP 3 To make the slipper top pattern, trace the sole pattern onto a piece of white paper. Draw a line approximately 1 1/2" (4 cm) beyond the top half of the sole pattern. Cut out.

4

5

STEP 4 Pencil a line ½" (1 cm) inside the curved front edge of the slipper top pattern. Cut into this line in several places (like making darts in a sewing project). Finish the slipper top with collage elements, sewing, fake jewels, feathers, etc. Cover the top sole with interesting paper; then glue slipper top onto top sole, carefully folding the paper and adjusting it to your foot. **STEP 5** Glue the slipper top/sole to the rest of the sole. Use tree tape (or any other sort of paper) on the outside of the sole for a finished look.

Chinese Flip-Flop

Cut out soles and heels as for shoe, but do not glue them together. Punch holes through the soles with the awl for a thong, which can be made out of duct tape. Thread the thong through the holes and then glue the layers together, covering as desired with decorative elements.

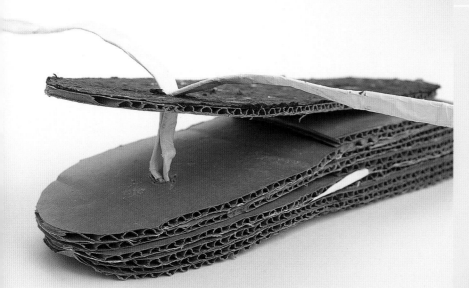

About the Paper

Very little handmade Chinese paper is exported to the West, but machine-made joss paper can be found in Chinatown shops. Machine-made joss paper is brightly colored and inexpensive. Thousands of sheets are burned on special occasions. Joss paper with images of money, clothes, and other necessities, and small squares with gold or silver foil in the middle, folded into a boat shape, are burned at funerals. Joss paper printed with Taoist symbols is used in celebrating the Chinese New Year.

In many parts of China, fiber is beaten by means of a foot-operated stamper. This photo was taken in the village of Bei Zhang, in Chang-an County, about 20 miles southwest of Xian.

making paper

Making paper is a magical experience that takes you back to the basics of paper craft. It is fun, easy, and rewarding, and requires only a few household items and readily available art supplies. Once you discover how quickly you can make beautiful paper from scraps of junk mail or papers in your recycling pile, you will find yourself with a growing stack of handmade papers to make into cards, wrapping paper, bookbinding, or any other project.

Most of the supplies you will need for making your own paper are already at hand. You will need a large shallow vat, such as a plastic wash basin or a cat litter box, a blender, and the material to make the paper. The best source for this is junk mail and other paper recycling that so easily collects at home. These used papers can be reduced down to paper pulp—a mixture of paper fibers and water—to produce fresh, new sheets of paper. To make existing paper into pulp, remove staples, cellophane, or other miscellaneous materials from the paper. Tear the paper into small pieces and soak in water to soften the fibers, making them easier to break down. Then put the soaked bits of paper into a blender, with water, to make into pulp.

The other supplies you will need to make paper are a deckle and mold, felts, and pressing boards, all of which can be found at artist's supply stores. The deckle and mold form and determine the size of the final sheet of paper. The deckle looks like a picture frame with a screen covering it. It captures the paper pulp, separating the fibers out from the water as it is removed from the vat. On top of the deckle is the mold, which shapes the sheet of paper. The deckle and the mold are slipped beneath the surface of the pulp in the vat and then lifted out, capturing the paper fibers while allowing the water to drain away.

After you remove the deckle and mold from the vat, you have what is essentially a very soggy piece of paper. To remove the moisture from the paper, press the sheet between felts and boards. The felts absorb some of the extra water, allow you to move the paper in progress from one workstation to another, and prevent the paper from sticking to the pressing boards. If you can't find felts, wool blankets cut to size work just as well. Press as much water as possible out of the sheet of paper. Then move it to a smooth surface, such as foam core, glass, or Formica, to dry.

Once you understand the basic papermaking techniques, you can easily produce numerous variations and styles of paper. At the pulp stage, add dyes to make colored papers, or mix in found objects such as petals, lace, or string to become an integral part of the paper. Add another sheet of handmade paper, or press shapes into the paper. To turn out larger sheets of paper, use larger deckles and molds and correspondingly bigger vats. If you do not have the room to set up a bigger vat, create larger sheets by overlapping smaller ones. After a sheet of paper has been placed on the pressing board, do not press it, but add another sheet of unpressed paper right next to and touching the first. Continue adding these unpressed sheets until the paper is the size you want, and then place the second felt and pressing board

on top of the paper and press as usual. The resulting sheet is a composite of all the smaller sheets you placed together.

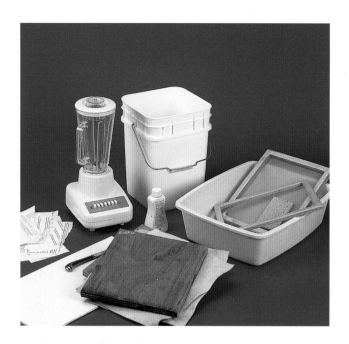

HOW TO
make paper

THIS RECIPE *for navy-colored paper is quick, easy, and produces beautiful results. To create a different color paper, simply substitute the blue dye with another color, or after you have made a few blue sheets of paper, add some yellow or red dye to the pulp to make either green or purple sheets of paper. Take your time, have fun, and experiment. The result will be your own unique papers you can use to add a more personal touch to your paper projects.*

Materials · paper scraps · blender · water · blue dye · large, shallow vat (large enough to contain deckle and mold) · 8 ¹/₂" x 11" (21.5 cm x 28 cm) deckle and mold · 2 pieces of felt just larger than the paper you are making · pressing boards · sheet of foam core or other smooth surface · towels and sponges · bucket · putty or butter knife

1

Tear the paper into small pieces, measuring no more than 1" (2.5 cm) square, and place them in the bucket. Add enough water to cover the paper and let it soak overnight to soften the fibers. The next day, put a small handful of the paper pieces into the blender with a little bit of water and blend until the pulp is smooth, with no lumps. It should resemble the consistency of cooked oatmeal. Repeat until all of the soaked paper bits have been made into pulp. Pour it all into the shallow vat and add several tablespoons of the blue dye until you have created a rich, blue-colored mixture.

2

Mix enough water into the pulp so that it has a soupy consistency (the more water you add to the pulp, the thinner the sheet of paper will be). Agitate the mixture to ensure an even dispersion of the pulp. Stack the mold on top of the deckle and, beginning at one side of the vat, slip the deckle and mold beneath the surface of the pulp solution in one smooth movement.

3

Lift the deckle and mold straight up out of the vat and gently shake them to ensure an even dispersion of the paper pulp. Allow as much water as possible to drain off, and remove the mold from the top of the deckle.

4

To prevent the pulp from sticking to the felts, soak them in water and then wring them out. Place one pressing board on the work surface with a piece of felt on top of it. In a quick, smooth motion flip, the deckle over onto the felt so that the sheet of paper you are forming is trapped between the screen of the deckle and the felt. With a towel or sponge, press against the screen of the deckle to squeeze out as much water from the pulp sheet as possible. Gently remove the deckle, leaving the pulp sheet on the felt. If the pulp starts to tear as you lift off the deckle, press out more water before continuing.

5

Lay the other felt on top of the pulp sheet and the other pressing board on top of that. Press the sheet firmly between the two boards to remove more water. You may find that standing on the boards is the easiest way to do this. Carefully remove the top board and felt.

6

Lift the felt that the sheet of paper is on and turn it over onto the foam core, pulp side down. Press the sheet against the foam core and gently peel the felt away from the sheet of paper. If the paper starts to tear, press it back against the foam to remove more moisture before continuing to peel off the felt. Leave the newly formed sheet of paper on the foam core for several hours to dry.

7

When the edges of the paper sheet start to pull away from the foam core and the center of the sheet feels dry to the touch, slip a putty or butter knife between the paper and the foam core and gently pry the paper from the surface.

PAPERMAKING TIPS

• To make your own deckle and mold set, use two matching picture frames and enough window screening (available at any hardware store) to cover the opening of one frame. Remove the glass, backing, and stands from the frames so that only the front portion of the frame remains. Wrap the screening around one frame and staple or glue it in place. This frame is now the deckle. Stack the other frame on top of the deckle to use it as the mold for your paper.

• Use cookie cutters as molds on top of a deckle to make small, fun-shaped pieces of paper to use for invitations or name tags.

• To make a thick sheet of paper, add only a little water to the pulp before forming the sheet. For a thin sheet of paper, dilute the pulp considerably with water.

ENVELOPE *templates*

The envelope patterns that follow correspond to the Special Occasion Invitations (see pg. 18). Make the envelope first to make sure that all the pieces fit inside—the invitation, response card, map, etc.

To create the Pamphlet Style Invitation, trace the A2 envelope shape onto the paper and cut out. Use the same pattern for the envelope liner. Trace the A6 envelope pattern for the Layered Invitation. To create the Wrapped Invitation, use the Square Envelope template.

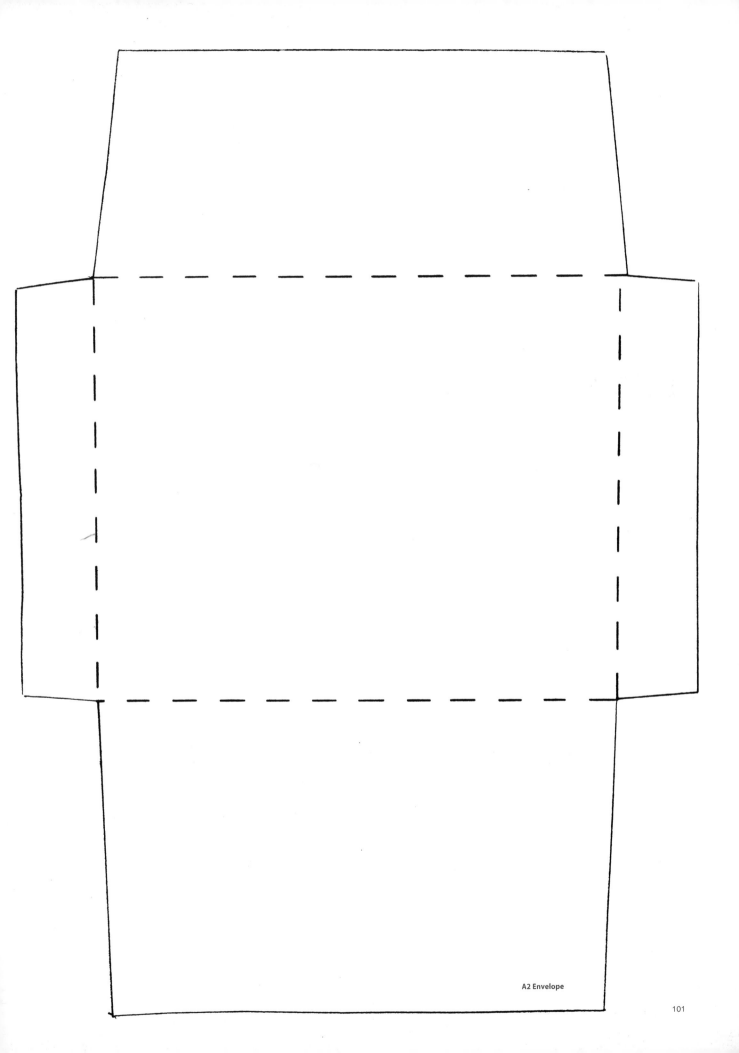

A2 Envelope

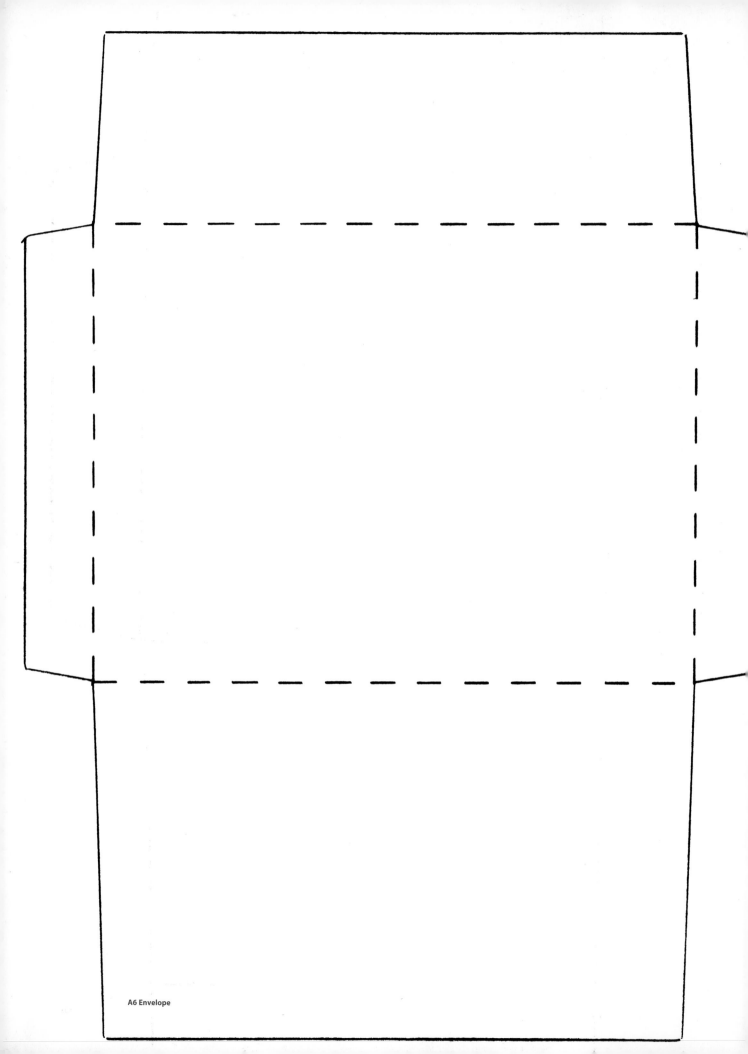

A6 Envelope

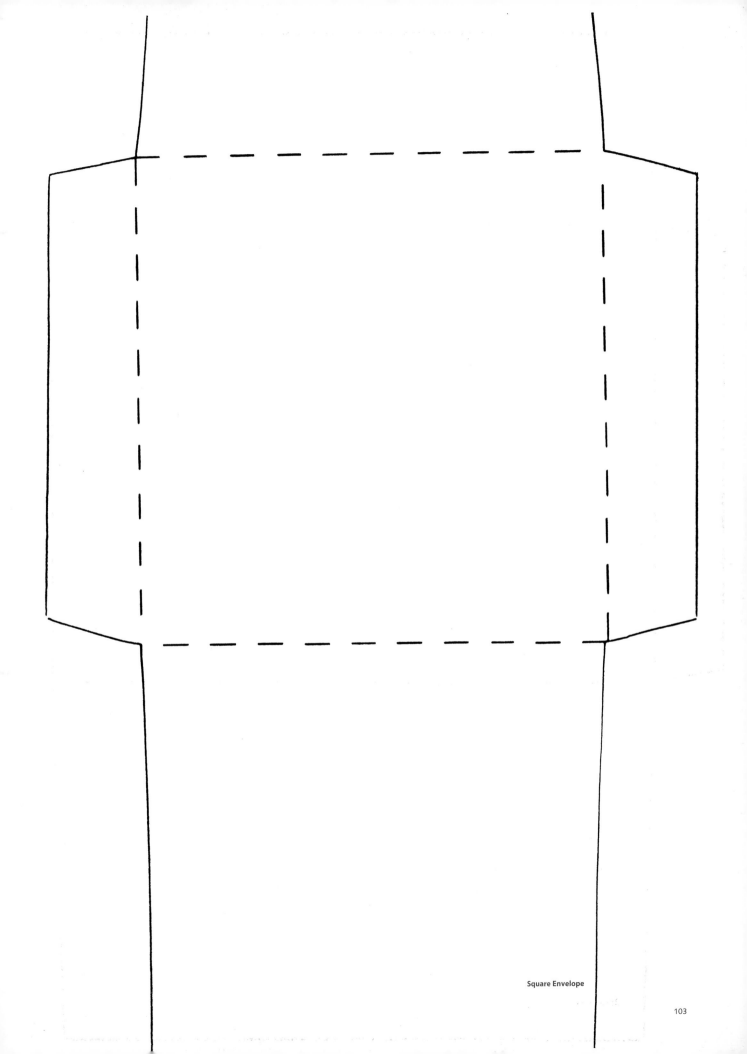

Square Envelope

resources

Handmade Papers and Art Supplies

Aiko's Art Materials Import, Inc.
3347 North Clark Street
Chicago, IL 60657
Phone: (312) 404-5600

Amsterdam Art
1013 University Avenue
Berkeley, CA 94710
Phone: (510) 649-4800

Daniel Smith
4150 First Avenue South
P.O. Box 84268
Seattle, WA 98124-5568
Phone: (800) 426-6740

Dick Blick
P.O. Box 1267
Galesburg, IL 61402-1267
Phone: (800) 447-8192

Kate's Paperie Soho
561 Broadway
New York, NY 10012
Phone: (212) 941-9816

New York Central Art Supply
62 Third Avenue
New York, NY 10003
Phone: (212) 473-7705

Paper Connection International
Lauren Pearlman
208 Pawtuxet Avenue
Cranston, RI 02905
Phone/Fax: (401) 461-2135

The Paper Crane
280 Cabot Street
Beverly, MA 01915
Phone: (978) 927-3131

Paper Source
232 W. Chicago Avenue
Chicago, IL 60610
Phone: (800) 248-8035
(also in Evanston, Kansas City,
Philadelphia & Cambridge)

Rugg Road Paper Company
105 Charles Street
Boston, MA 02114
Phone: (617) 742-0002 Fax: (617) 742-0008

Papermaking Supplies

Carriage House Paper/New York
79 Guernsey Street
Brooklyn, NY 11222
Phone/Fax: (718) 599-7857

David Reina Designs, Inc.
79 Guernsey Street
Brooklyn, NY 11222
Phone: (718) 599-1237 Fax: (718) 599-7857

Dieu Donné Papermill, Inc.
433 Broome Street
New York, NY 10013
Phone: (212) 226-0573 Fax: (212) 226-6088
E-mail: ddpaper@cybernex.net

Fascinating Folds
Phone: (800) 968-2418
E-mail: sales@fascinating-folds.com

Gold's Artworks Inc.
2100 North Pine Street
Lumberton, NC 28358
Phone: (919) 739-9605

Arnold Grummer's Papermaking Supplies
c/o Greg Markim, Inc.
P.O. Box 13245
Milwaukee, WI 53213
Phone: (800) 453-1485

Lee Scott McDonald, Inc.
P.O. Box 264
Charlestown, MA 02129
Phone: (617) 242-2505 Fax: (617) 242-8825

Magnolia
2527 Magnolia Street
Oakland, CA 94607
Phone: (510) 839-5268 Fax: (510) 893-8334

The Papertrail
170 University Avenue West
Waterloo, Ontario
Canada N2L 3E9
Phone: (800) 421-6826 Fax: (519) 884-9655

Timothy Moore Paper Molds and Bookbinding Tools
14450 Behling Road
Concord, MI 49237
Phone: (617) 524-6318

Twinrocker
P.O. Box 413
Brookston, IN 47923
Phone: (800) 757-8946

Periodicals

Hand Papermaking
P.O. Box 77027
Washington, DC 20013-7027
Phone: (800) 821-6604

Organizations

Friends of Dard Hunter
P.O. Box 773
Lake Oswego, OR 97034

IAPMA (International Association of
Hand Papermakers and Paper Artists)
Anne Vilsboll, President
Fredensgade 4
Stryno, Ryudkobing
DK-5900 Denmark

Websites

The World Wide Web is a great resource for finding handmade paper. Below are a few websites to get started on your search for more information.

Fascinating Folds
An extensive website featuring supplies and reference materials for paper art and crafts.
http://www.fascinating-folds.com

Fine Paper Company
Handmade & tree-free papers; letterpress printing
http://www.finepaperco.com

Oblation Papers & Press
Handmade papers and workshops
http://www.oblationpapers.com

Paper Connection International
Wide selection of Japanese papers
http://www.paperconnection.com

The Paper Crane
Handmade paper, exhibits & workshops
http://www.papercrane.com

index

Acknowledgments

Many people have been very generous with their time, knowledge, photographs, and encouragement in support of this project, but the author wishes to especially thank the following people for their help:

Lynn Amlie at the University of Iowa Center for the Book; Karen Andreas at The School for Field Studies; Tom Bannister, Managing Director of the periodical *Hand Papermaking*; friend and photographer Martha Everson; Jane M. Farmer of Paper Road/Tibet; Jim Fox of Imports Unlimited; Christina Hellmich, Director of Collections Management at the Peabody Essex Museum; Elaine and Sidney Koretsky, paper couple extraordinaire; the cheerful and intelligent staff at Rockport Publishers; Rick Sorenson; Brian Thomas; my husband, Mike, for his loving support; and my son, Will, for his willingness to eat take-out food.

About the Author

Gail Hercher, B.F.A., M.F.A., a paper artist and teacher, is the owner of The Paper Crane, a studio/gallery in Beverly, Massachusetts, that offers exhibits, workshops, and supplies for the paper arts. She has taught for more than 20 years in schools, museums, and colleges and currently gives workshops throughout New England and at The Paper Crane and Montserrat College of Art.

She has served as a visiting artist at many locations including, The Newport Art Museum (R.I.), Temari Center for Asian and Pacific Arts (Hawaii), The Black Ships Festival, The Vermont Alliance for Arts Education, and is on the Event and Residency Roster of the Massachusetts Cultural Council. She exhibits her work and has received several awards and grants, including a Fulbright Fellowship to study in Europe.